Piano Development
L7

Composed by Giovanni Andreani

First published in 2023 by
GA
Via Colombo 4, 24061 Albano Sant'Alessandro, BG, Italy
Copyright © Giovanni Andreani 2017

ISBN 978-88-314710-3-9

To Cristina Airoldi

an ever shining soul, who enlightened me

on the intrinsic value of the meaning of holism

"Music is a manifestation of the human spirit, similar to language. Its greatest practitioners have conveyed to mankind things not possible to say in any other language"

— Zoltán Kodály

PREFACE

A comprehensive and effective programme must consider all of the possible sectors in which the student's skills and competence can develop, which fall into two main categories: musicianship[1] and instrumental skills. The Music Method Project (MusMP) comprises the Piano Method Project (PMP), related to the development of instrumental skills, and the Musicianship Method Project (MMP), related to musicianship development.

While musicianship will develop slightly when studying an instrument, scientifically well-programmed musicianship development will be the primary factor for excellent instrumental improvement. As a consequence, some areas of development in PMP will be performed at the piano while others will have to be undertaken with or without the subsidiary use of a piano (see footnote n. 2).

The more the proposed activities are varied and systematically organised, the better the development of skills and competence will be. As a consequence, the contrast between different activities will stimulate the student's interest, which will result in greater emotional involvement, a higher level of participation, and a more dynamic attitude.

Differentiation must also consider the time terms that are intrinsic to all specific Development Areas.

In PMP, the following time terms have been conceived:

- Instant Term [IT] - from 5 seconds to 15 minutes
- Daily Term [DT] - 15 minutes to 6 hours
- Very Short Term [VST] - 1 day to 1 week
- Short Term [ST] – 2 weeks
- Medium Term [MT] – 1 month
- Long Term [LT] – 2 to 4 months
- Very Long Term [VLT] – 4 to 6 months

Within a well-differentiated programme, the student should deal simultaneously with activities that require different time terms that derive from different areas. Short-term activities should outnumber those that are expected to take longer.

---

1   Musicianship should be considered essential for the student's improvement; in many cases it is not, for many reasons, among which lies the complexity to plan a specific curriculum.

Although it is undoubtedly important for the student to simultaneously manage various activities as part of the different areas of development, any new activity should be gradually introduced.

Within PMP, Piano Development (PD) is the only area that should be constantly active: all other areas can be started according to the teacher's discretion, in relation to the student's aptitude, specific needs, expectations, and so forth.

In PMP, the Development Areas are (with their corresponding time terms):

- Piano Development [VST]
- Sing & Play[2] [VST]
- Note Reading[2] [IT] – [VST]
- Listen & Play[2] [IT] – [VST]
- Sight Reading [IT]
- Technique Exercises [ST] – [VLT]
- Scales & Arpeggios [ST] – [VLT]
- Études [MT] – [VLT]
- Quick Studies [IT]
- Piano Improvisation [IT] – [VST]
- Piano Composition [VST] – [MT]
- Solo Repertoire [MT] – [VLT]
- Piano Duet Repertoire [MT] – [VLT]
- Chamber Music Repertoire [MT] – [VLT]

Some activities will be achieved after a very short time whereas others will require longer. Moreover, after some activities have been attained, a maintenance programme will be necessary: this is true for some technical exercises, scales, and arpeggios, and some selected études and repertoire pieces, etc.

---

2   Transitional areas of correlation between Musicianship and Instrumental Development.

INTRODUCTION

Piano Development (PD) is, throughout the PMP Development Areas, the main framework around which all other Development Areas orbit; it has been conceived to help piano teachers achieve a profound view of their student's improvements while guiding them throughout the higher levels of piano playing.

PD is divided into a first set of 20 levels and the student should be working on two different and consecutive levels at the same time.

As progress is made, a new Development Area may be added: the more areas the student manages, the more profoundly competence and skills will grow; nonetheless, PD should be the only Development Area on which the student will be working constantly.

PD consists of short pieces that the student will have to prepare for the following lesson; how these pieces will be mastered is an issue to be pre-emptively clarified in order to positively monitor the student's progress. Therefore, the teacher will have to determine in advance which criteria to adopt when evaluating each piece and assigning a new one in its place. Criteria for when to pass from one level to another should also be established in advance.

The general complexity expressed at each level of PD does not have to be comparable to the difficulty of other areas simultaneously studied, especially if related to repertoire. Indeed, the student may find him/herself studying a repertoire piece that is much more difficult than is expressed by the level required in PD: this would be perfectly appropriate while the contrary would, surely be unfitting. The time term of PD is classified as VST while a repertoire piece may be classified from MT to VLT; therefore, the latter can be more complex.

Using this Book

There is no strict way in which to use this book; it can be adopted for various purposes accordingly. Nevertheless, its main purpose is to be part of the PMP. The teacher who wishes to follow the PMP principles will find a rich collection of musical material, all PMP resources were also conceived within a specific plan inherently designed into an effective and comprehensive programme.

The main characteristic that distinguishes this level is related to the variety of textures expressed throughout the pieces in this book, rather than an increasing rhythmic complexity within the progression of each piece's melodic line. In such a sense, the student will be dealing with different textures, derived by combining each melodic line with various, distinct, structures, thus favouring diverse contrasts between the melodies and their underlying parts.

All pieces in this book will require the use of both hands playing simultaneously. The pieces are proposed in cicles of sets of five, and, while following one another, the texture will be perceived as gradually increasing in its thickness and complexity, by means af a gradual contrapunctual use of the musical lines and harmony involved. Each new set of pieces will begin with a rarefied texture, thus favouring the principle of diversification.

By following the PMP principles the student will be working on PD L6 or PD L8 together with this level; in such a case the student will be dealing with a mixed set of pieces composed for two hands playing simultaneously as well as pieces for two hands performing one only melody (in the case of using PD L6 together with this book), or pieces exclusively for two hands playing simultaneously (in the case of using PD L8 together with this book).

Rhythm

At this level, rhythmic patterns and durations do no longer need to be introduced; in addition to the previous level, only the following rhythmic patterns will be found:

Notes and Hand-Positions

The student should be able to find and play any key in any octave by matching the key's name (or names) with its position on the keyboard.

The student should be able to name the notes from the staff with both the G clef and the F clef; reading fluently is not required for starting this level, as it is the ability to determine the first note of each piece that is needed (the 'Note Reading' series may be carried out contextually to improve pure note-reading skills).

At this level, all pieces are composed using mainly five notes per hand; by avoiding the use of a unique type of five-finger position, various intervals between the notes will occur, generating a variety of hand positions, from a squeezed penta-chromatic position to a more common five finger position, to wider positions and, in some cases, to the use of extended positions[1]. Each hand position will be maintained throughout the piece. In some cases the melodies (mainly composed on a prefixed set of five notes) will appear enhanced by the use of chromatic neighbour notes. In such a case, by analising the piece prior to performing it, the student - with the teacher's assistance - should be able to extrapolate the notes belonging to the main structure. This utmost significant practice will lead to a profound understanding of the roles embodied in each, single note, thus favouring a more, eventually, desired and spontaneous interpretation within the melodic profile of the pieces contained in this book. Besides, this attitude will also stand out when dealing with any other piece.

Let's consider, for example, a set of five notes, identifiable as degrees 1, 2, 3, 4, 5 of a major pentachord representing the main structure of a melody; within this main set, the second and fourth degree also appear higher in pitch by one semitone, acting as chromatic neighbour notes of the third and fifth degrees respectively. By identifying the five main notes while excluding the neighbour notes, the student will be able to visualise the required hand position; in many cases, the same fingers will be used for matching the notes that will be also altered as chromatic neighbour notes. Ultimately, a five finger position will be considered as such, regardless of the overall quantity of notes determined by the use of chromatic neighbour notes.

Fingering

The student should be able to understand and adopt fingering indications; although at this level, all pieces are composed using mainly five notes per hand[2], various intervals between the notes and different combinations of fingers will occur.

Time Signatures

At this level, the following time signatures will be found:

---

1   An extended position occurs when the hand needs to leap for reaching a single note, out of range in comparison with the initial, or main position. There is no way for strictly defining such a hand position: some hands will comfortably reach and include a note within a tenth from the lower of the overall notes in the hand position, while others will have to consider leaping for including a note enclosed by an octave from the lower of the overall notes within the hand position.

2   In some piece more than five notes per hand are required to be played; in these cases the main melodic structure is indeed composed by five notes while the remaining ones will be chromatic neighbour notes.

Among the proposed time signatures, so called irregular time signatures (also known as Bulgarian rhythm[3]) will develop a strong rhythmic control, and a profound sense of metre[4]. The non regular alternation of groups of two and three (as it occurs in pieces nos. 13, 21, 27, 34, 55) will further develop such ability, and competence. Time changes within the same piece (as it occurs in pieces nos. 13, 34, 37, 43, 48[5], 54) will further contribute to a profound development of a sense of metre.

Some Teaching Directions

All starting notes should be identified and labelled; when doing so, the octave number should always be included: there are several methods that combine note names and pitch octave numbers; in 'Scientific Pitch Notation' (SPN), for example, so-called 'middle C' is combined with the number 4 to identify its pitch octave, thus defining the note as C_4[6]. When assigning a new piece, the student should attempt to identify and label the starting note with the teacher's assistance.

Methodological Approach to these Pieces

It must be remembered that preparation for playing a piece must involve the issues that the student will have to deal with when practising alone without the teacher's support; at this level, solving preparation problems requires answering the following four questions, as it can be seen in Fig. 1:

I. Which hand begins playing the main theme? And what type of melodic or harmonic structure is played by the other hand?

II. Which is the starting note for each hand?

III.

---

3   'Bulgarian Rhythm' defines a metre, found in folk music from the Balkans, East Europe up to the foothills of the Middle East. In notated classical music it has been schematised by groping beats that subdivide into 2 and 3 common values, also known as 'irregular' time or 'odd time'.

4   One fundamental PMP's principle is to distinguish 'Time Signature' from 'Metre'. While the time signature acts as a visual frame of reference, within which the beats are organised in groups, metre is specific to a perceptual phenomenon, not always in line with what one would expect by merely interpreting the time signature. For example, a hemiolia, occurring in a duple compound time, will be perceived as a simple ternary time. There are numerous examples in music literature of all times where the metre stands out in conflict with the time signature. As a further instance, beside many others, it is not uncommon to find the re-exposure of a theme - such as in Scarlatti's sonatas, for example - placed in a different part of the measure compared to a previous exposition.

Justin London, in 'Hearing in Time: Psychological Aspects of Musical Meter' refers to metre as follows: "[Metre] involves our initial perception as well as subsequent anticipation of a series of beats that we abstract from the rhythm surface of the music as it unfolds in time".

5   In piece no. 48, the three quavers (or eighth notes) in measures 2, 4, 6, 8_1, 8_2, must be performed in time of a beat of the previos measure, thus resulting as a triplet equal intime to that specific beat.

6   In some countries C_4 is named C_3 or other pitch notation systems may be adopted.

IV. Which finger plays each starting note?

V. Which other notes/fingers are required to be played? Are there any neighbour notes[7] within the two parts?

All four of these points should never be taken for granted and, when solved, preparation will be complete and the hand-positions obtained: the student will now be ready to perform the piece and concentrate on another set of details while playing.

Fig. 1

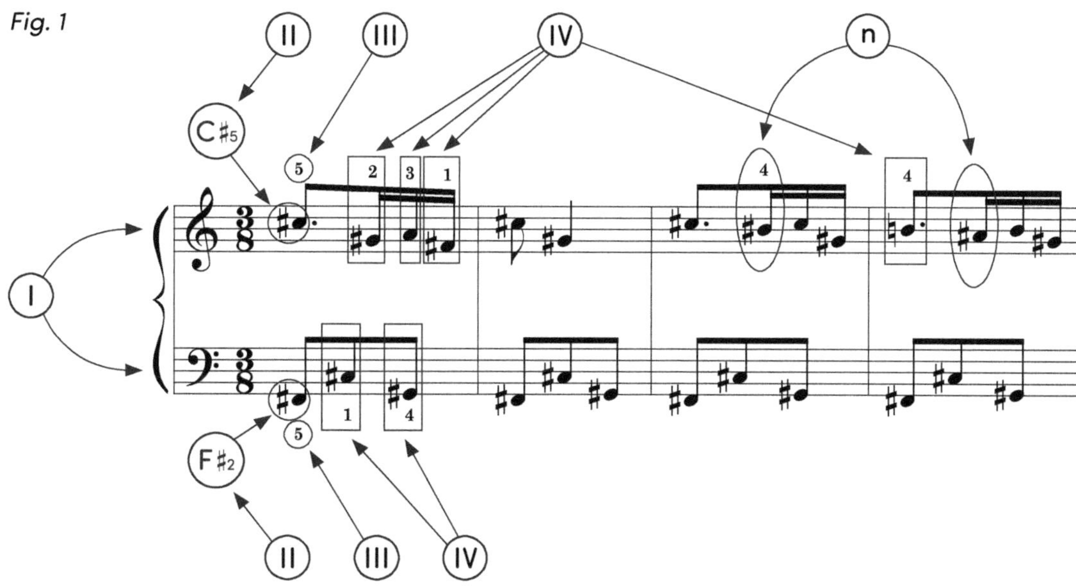

To facilitate adaptation to the required hand positions, before attempting to play the piece, the student may improvise some short motifs, as shown in Figs. 2 [A], [B], [C], [D], [E] (considering, for example, the piece as in Fig. 1):

Fig. 2

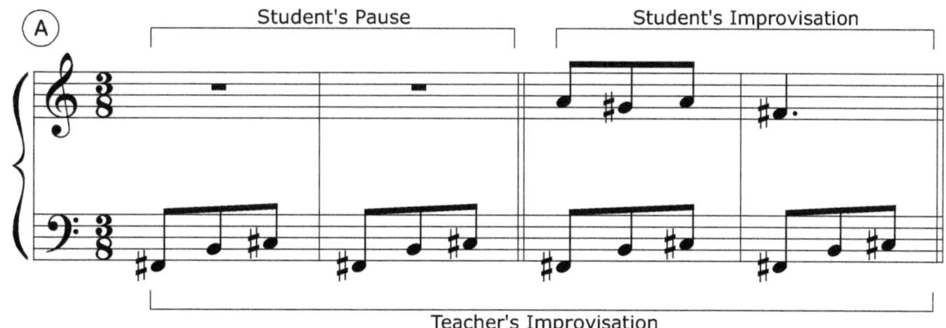

---

7 Neighbour notes in Fig. 1 are labelled with the letter 'n'.

Fig. 2A - The student, after having identified which hand performs the main theme, improvises a simple motif on a fixed length (in this case of two measures), taking care to rest for a number of measures equal to the improvised section, before improvising again[8]. In this way, the student will be able to concentrate on short, full meaningful melodic motifs, without having to struggle in creating long phrases. Furthermore, a profound sense of metre will develop in relation to the control required during the measures in which the student will be resting and preparing for a new improvisation.

The student improvises a series of motifs while the teacher plays the underlying part throughout, without interruption; although it is not necessary to propose the exact underlying part, it is indeed important to play a same kind of structure, as observed in the piece. This analytical process will stimulate an attitude to observing in a much profound way the structural elements within a piece.

Fig. 2

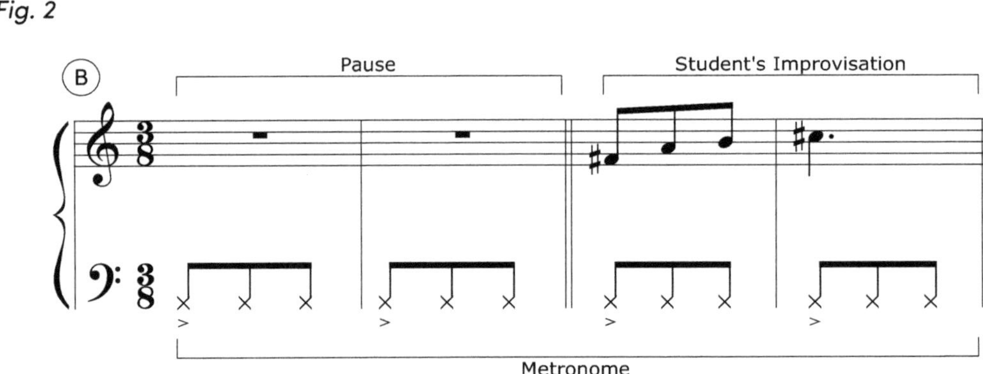

Fig. 2B - The student, while practicing alone, can adopt the same practice as described in Fig. 2A by playing together with a metronome: in this case, the metronome will prove to be a helpful resource for outlining - during the pauses between each improvisation - the metre itself, rather than requiring the student to 'keep in time' during his/her improvisation. Modern metronomes are capable of emphasising primary and secondary beats, therefore, the metronome, when appropriately set, will turn to be considerably helpful in such a sense.

---

8   It is mostly important to begin each improvising session starting from the pausing section: in such a way, the student will be initially pervaded by the overall length of each motif, and also feel and be aware of the metre subtended.

Fig. 2

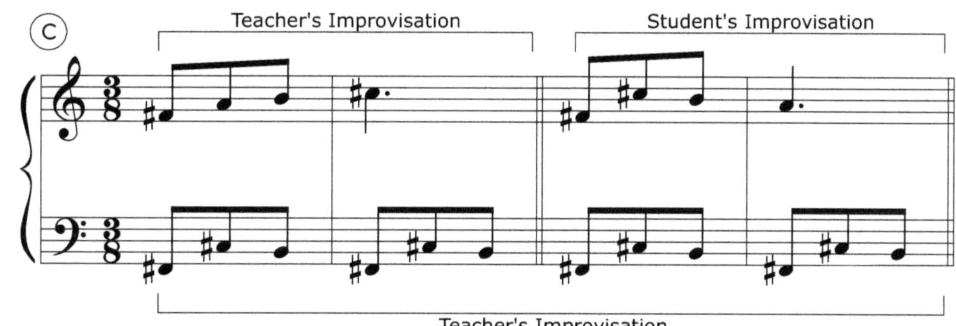

Fig. 2C[9] - The Teacher alternates improvised motifs with the student, while playing the whole underlying part. This practice is of the utmost importance due to the strong interaction involving the two performers: while the teacher's view of the student's abilities will be favoured in a distinctive, remarkable, holistic way, the student, from his/her point of perception, will constantly be pervaded by a positive stimulus for which every motif's element - from the melodic shaping, to the articulations, rhythm, dynamics, tempo, and many other less definable elements - will tend to rise.

Fig. 2

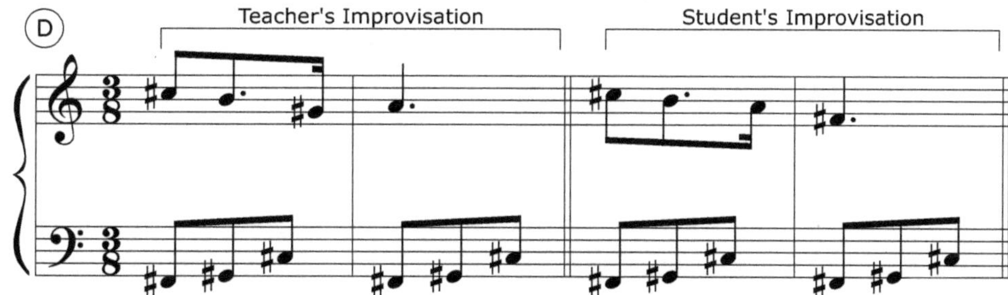

Fig. 2D - The Teacher alternates improvised motifs with the student, each playing their own underlying part. The student, at this stage, will gradually increase the ability to coordinate the two parts simultaneously, while improvising the melodic line. The underlying part should be the same for teacher and student, and be maintained throughout the entire improvisation, unless it's a non predictable part, such as an independent second voice.

---

9   The improvisation activity as described in Fig. 2C can be proposed as the very first improvising stage instead of beginning with the activity as described in Fig. 2A, while the activity as described in Fig. 2B will result suitable for the student while practicing alone.

Fig. 2

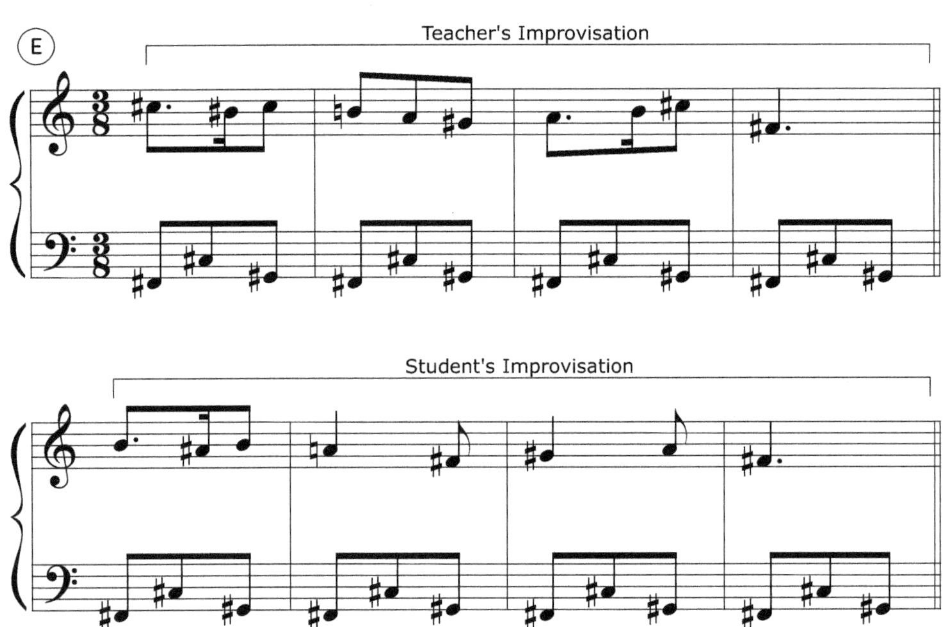

Fig. 2E - Improvising with the use of neighbour notes should take place at a further stage, steering clear to avoid their use before having identified and improvised by playing the only notes forming the main melodic structure. Neighbour chromatic notes should appear non as passing notes[10], while leading to their landing note from which the melodic profile previously departed. Once again, the student, by playing alternately with the teacher, will constantly be exposed to an effective and stimulating practice, which will guarantee a crucial support to any eventual theoretical analysis.

Accidentals

Although, at the very first stage, it is not necessary to introduce the full meaning of symbols such as the sharp, the flat, and the natural, the student may, at this level, already be aware of the specific meaning of these symbols[11]. Double sharps and double flats may not be introduced while beginning this level, although some do occur further in this book. The specific meaning of these symbols may eventually be introduced later on, according to the theory programme adopted.

---

10   An exeption to this rule are the notes E♯ (in measure no. 7) and C in piece no. 26 and the note E in the second to last measure in piece no. 49.

11   As the student begins to learn to link, for example, the note name G with a specific key on the keyboard, the same can be done for keys named G♯ and A♭, etc. This linking may also include C♭-B, B♯-C, F♭-E and E♯-F note/key combinations.

More on Hand Positions

A fundamental pedagogical principle proposed here is to avoid imposing a C-centred hand position as standard, while also steering clear of favouring one single clef over the other; the use of just a few hand-positions is also avoided. The student will be exploring the whole keyboard while gradually experiencing a variety of different hand-positions.

This approach should not discourage those teachers who are used to only one or a few positions for a long term: having reached the minimum prerequisites recommended for adopting this textbook, the only main issue when assigning a new piece will be to identify, for each hand, the starting note and the finger associated with it; by finding the remaining notes and their finger combinations, the required hand positions will be assumed. One important advantage is that the hands will be able to assume different kinds of positions, from those with fingers covering only the white keys, to those with the hand pushed in a forward position and the fingers inserted between the black keys, up to those with the hand in a stretched position or in a squeezed, compressed position, among others. By constantly finding various new hand positions, the student will develop remarkable mental agility and improved equilibrium within his/her physical relationship with the keyboard.

Metronome

Metronome marks mainly suggest the pace at which a piece should be played. Playing in time to a metronome, however, is much more difficult than it may seem; it may be more productive to play duets in order to practise a fluent and uniform pace. When playing with a metronome, the student is required to constantly adjust his/her own pace to match the metronome's pulse whereas, when playing with another person, the adjustment is mutual.

Improvising Chamber Music

We encourage all teachers to improvise duets with their students as an alternative way of playing these and other pieces. Improvised duets may not only be performed as a three or four hand piano ensemble: once the student is able to play a piece from this series, improvising duets with alternative kinds of instruments, including percussion instruments and the use of the voice, among others, should always be encouraged. Changing roles is also important: the teacher or another student can play the piece while the student improvises an accompaniment or another musical structure; it is important, in some cases, to use an instrument easy to play, such a percussion instrument, for example.

Key Signatures

At this level, the majority of the pieces are presented without a key signature; most of them, however, are not related to C major or its relative minor key: accidentals, therefore, will appear for the moment, 'in itinere', for three reasons: the first is to accustom the student to key alterations, making them clear every time they are needed; the second reason is that these pieces, despite the fact they are mostly tonally identifiable, are nevertheless composed of only a small number of notes: it would then be possible to play a piece in D minor, for example, without ever having to play a B flat; and, thirdly, the student, in having to experience many possible hand positions, should be offered the opportunity to play, for example, in the key of E♭ minor, or any other key without having to know all the rules underlying the tonal structures. Nontheless, pieces with a key signature are gradually and sistematically introduced.

Directions for the Teacher

Each assigned piece should be prepared and played in its entirety and fully mastered for the next lesson (usually the following week); although at this level all pieces are required to be performed with both hands playing simultaneously, the teacher may require the student to just prepare and play the main melody and add the second part as an objective for a further lesson; nevertheless, one of the criteria to take into consideration is the development of the ability for immediately playing the two parts simultaneously; all preparing activities previously described will surely guide the student to an effective development of control and coordination, which are the focus within the pedagogical objectives determined for this level.

When assigning a new piece, the student and teacher together should pinpoint the first notes played by each hand and write them down with their pitch octave number; other notes may also be labelled if they lie in an extended hand-position. No other note names should be written down.

Finger numbers are provided for the hand to be situated in a particular position, when a new finger is needed, or when a new hand position occurs. No other finger numbers should be added. If the teacher decides to require different fingering this should be clearly established before assigning the work.

The student, when following these procedures alone, while practising, should be able to solve all problems related to the preparation of the piece, and know how to interpret all involved rhythmic patterns, durations, and time signatures included therein; consequently, the student should be able, by practising during the period until the following lesson, to perform the piece with a high degree of competency.

Moving to a New Piece

When evaluating whether a piece is to be considered as having been mastered and therefore archived and replaced by another one, a set of criteria should be considered as evaluating parameters; according to each student's poise, level of musicianship, general aptitude, and so forth, more or fewer criteria may be considered.

The main mandatory criteria could be:

- The piece must be played with flow and no interruption
- Rhythms and durations must be accurate
- Notes must be correct
- Fingers must be respected
- Playing should be realised in a relaxed and anxiety-free way

Further criteria that may apply according to the teacher's discretion, could be, among others:

- Hairpin diminuendos should be respected
- Dynamics and crescendo hairpins should be respected
- Articulation and accent signs should be respected
- The tempo may not be accurate as indicated, although the mood and the tempo itself should be appropriate to the style of the piece
- Phrasing and a sense of metre should be expressed

Once established, the criteria chosen for evaluating all performances must be strictly maintained throughout the level; if the student's performance does not meet the predetermined criteria, the piece should remain as an objective for the next lesson; when the performance meets the established criteria for a positive evaluation, the piece will be archived and replaced by one within the same level.

Moving to a New Level

Although it is always the teacher who plans and is responsible for the proposed programme, if the PMP principles are being followed, PD should be adopted by using two consecutive levels simultaneously.

When selecting a level for the first time, the teacher will identify the most appropriate stage for the student. The student will then begin from the level previous to that selected and, after the first few pieces have been studied, the first chosen level may be added: the student will therefore be simultaneously working on two consecutive levels.

The number of pieces assigned from each level should comprise more from the lower of the two levels while maintaining the following proportions:

Piano Development Weekly Assigned Work (no. of pieces)				
Task Type	*Pieces from Lower Level*	*Pieces from Higher Level*	*Total Pieces Assigned*	*Pieces Evaluated Weekly*
Light	1	1	2	1
Medium	2	1	3	1 or 2
Intense	3	1 or 2	4 or 5	2 or 3
Demanding	4	2	6	2 to 4

It is important to not evaluate all assigned pieces at each lesson: as a consequence, the non-played pieces will settle within the time before the next lesson; this is an important issue due to the fact that not all of the pieces may be well prepared for every following lesson, for different reasons, that are not always dependent on the student's diligence.

Three pieces are a sizeable task to deal with within a week, considering that each lesson will include activities from other areas as well; we therefore recommend assigning this number of pieces, as a medium task, as can be seen in the above table.

Before evaluating whether a student can move to the next level, at least the first 20 pieces should be practised.

If the student is consistently dealing with between one and three pieces (medium task), then a basic set consisting of at least the first 25 pieces should be practised before evaluating whether the student can move to the next level.

If the student is consistently dealing with more than three pieces (intense or demanding task), then a basic set consisting of at least the first 30 pieces should be practised before evaluating whether the student can move to the next level.

After having completed the defined set of pieces required before evaluating whether the student can move to the next level, the teacher should then use a predetermined criterion to evaluate whether such a condition exists; two procedures, among other possible solutions, are described here (for the case of a student dealing with a medium task):

Example 1: from piece 25, the teacher analyses the last five archived pieces and, when the average percentage of the positively performed pieces on the first required occasion is at least equal to 80%, the student will move to the next level.

Example 2: from piece 25, the teacher analyses the last four archived pieces and, when the last four pieces in a row are evaluated as positively performed on the first required occasion, the student will move to the next level.

As stated before, the majority of pieces assigned should be from the lower of the two levels, from which the student will move to a piece that is two levels ahead.

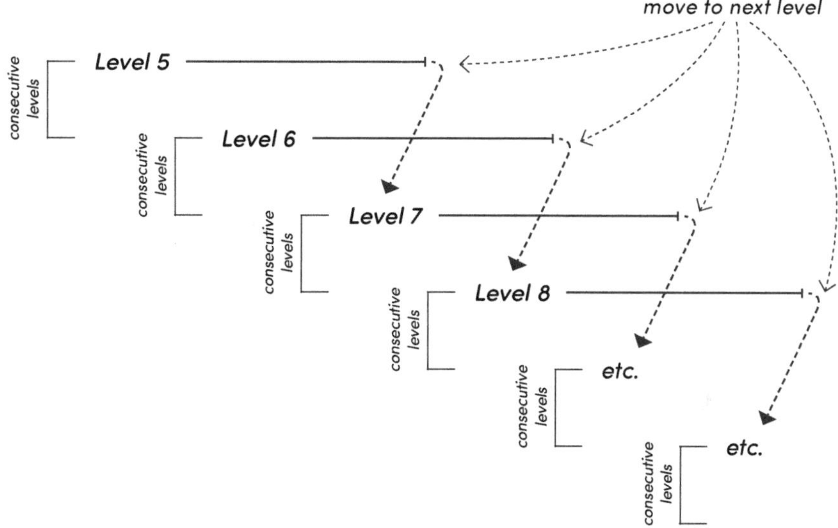

Monitoring

The teacher should keep a detailed record of all activities carried out at each lesson; this will provide an important amount of data that will make the teacher aware of the student's progress and improvements.

Although the teacher may select and assign a new piece according to a personal order, it is important to do so in the correct numerical order. All pieces are set into groups, each of which contains specific details or particular aspects that will recur cyclically.

Although the pieces will never all be at exactly the same level of difficulty, they are conceived to meet characteristics that will distinguish them as part of the specific level defined by this book.

LIST OF ABBREVIATIONS

MusMP: Music Method Project, which includes MMP and IMP

MMP: Musicianship Method Project

IMP: Instrumental Method Project

PMP: Piano Method Project, a part of IMP

PD: Piano Development, a Development Area of PMP

Development Area: a branch, a sector in which specific skills are developed

Activity: a piece, an exercise, anything from a one-bar rhythm to a whole movement of a sonata or anything else, provided that it is a whole defined item. An activity is part of a specific Development Area

Objective: a specific task intended to be accomplished according to a predetermined period of time. An objective is a part of or can coincide with an entire activity[12]

Duration[13]: any rhythmic value equal to or greater than the pulse value

Rhythmic pattern: a sequence of rhythmic values usually smaller than the pulse value and perceived as a structure generally fitting one[14] pulse

---

12   As an example, a thirty-two bar piece is divided in two sections of sixteen bars each: only one section is required to be studied for the time arranged with the student. In this case the whole piece is the activity while the single section is the objective. Let's say that in addition to the piece's section, one scale, one arpeggio and one study are also assigned: all of these are different objectives from activities from different development areas.

13   Duration also refers to the lenght of time of a piece.

14   Rhythmic patterns may also fit multiple beat durations; the most common ones, however, fit one or two beats.

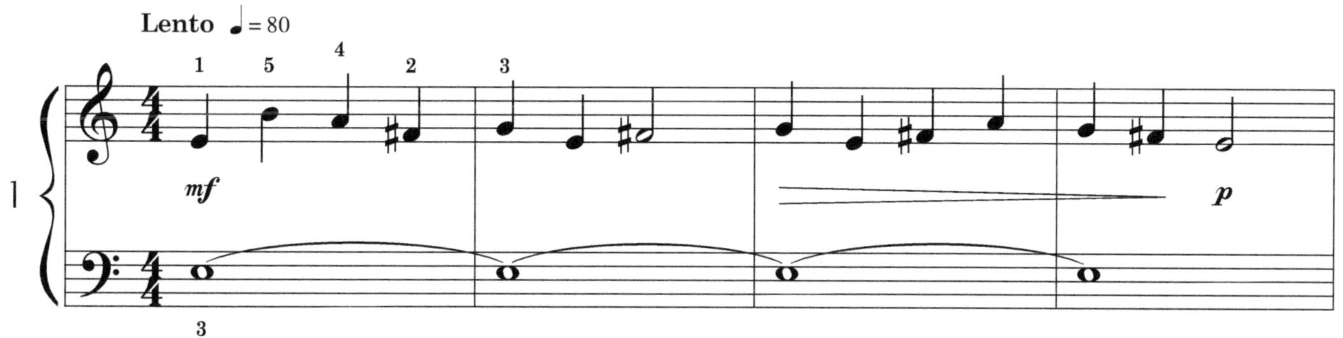

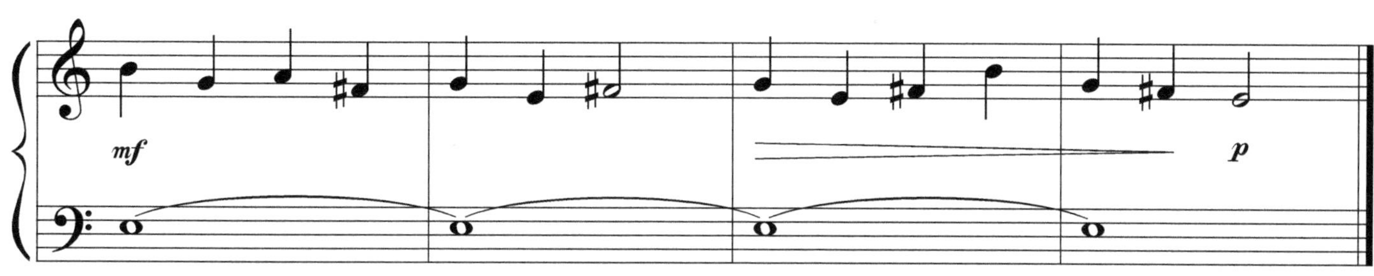

GA 22040

GA 22040

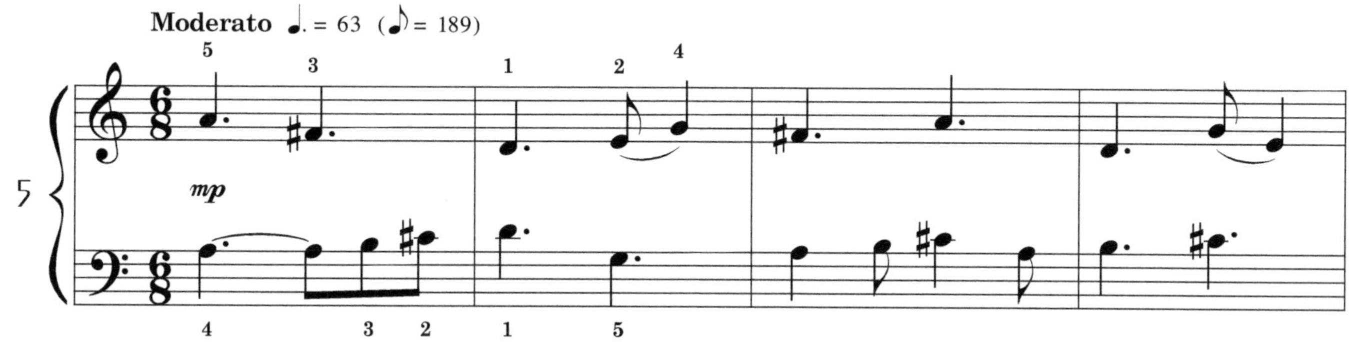

Moderato ♩. = 63 (♪ = 189)
mp
5

Allegretto ♩. = 70 (♪ = 210)
mp
f
6

Allegro ♪ = 252
7
mf
5
1

%
f

D.C. al % alla Coda   Coda
p   f   f

Allegro ♩ = 144
8
mf
1
5

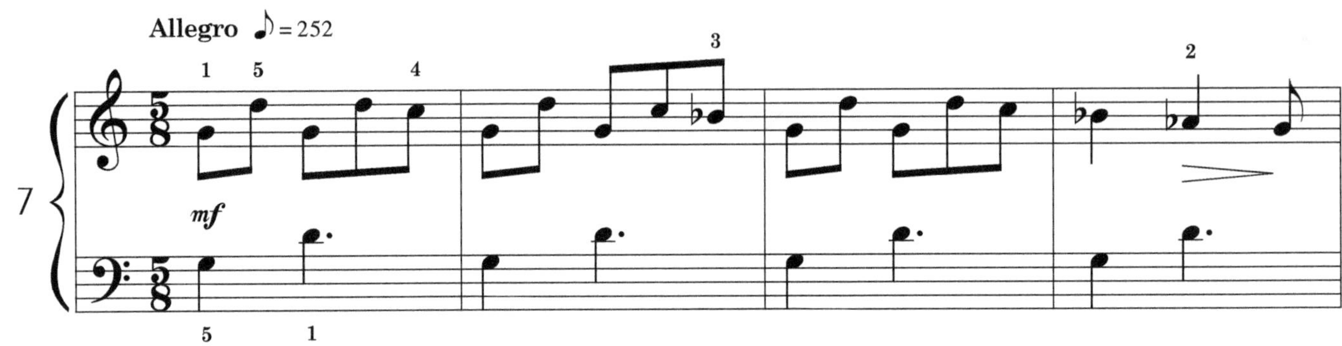

GA 22040

5
mp
Lento ♩. = 56 (♪ = 168) 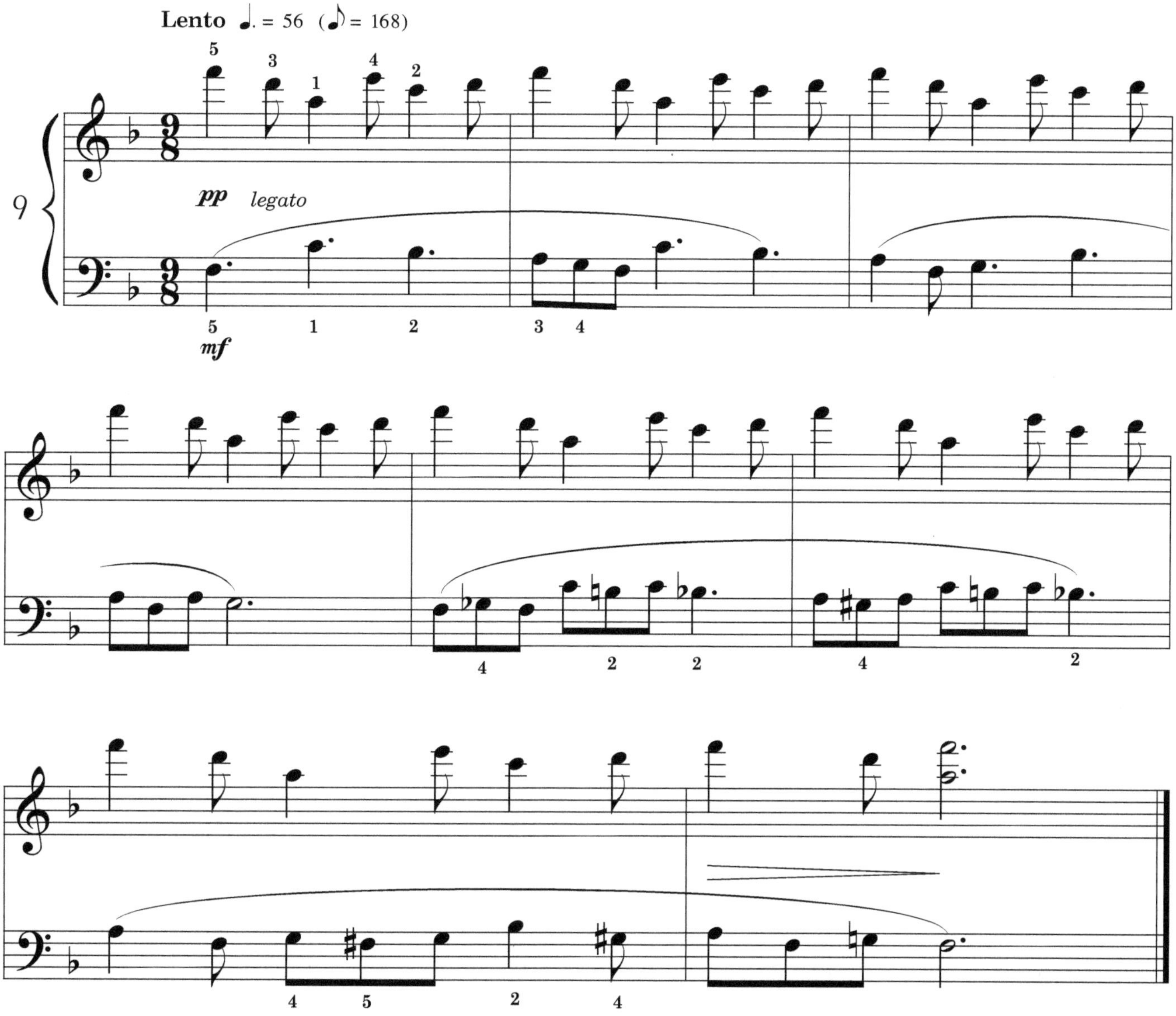
5 3 1 4 2
pp legato
9
5 1 2 3 4
mf
4 2 2 4 2
4 5 2 4

GA 22040

Moderatamente
mf

GA 22040

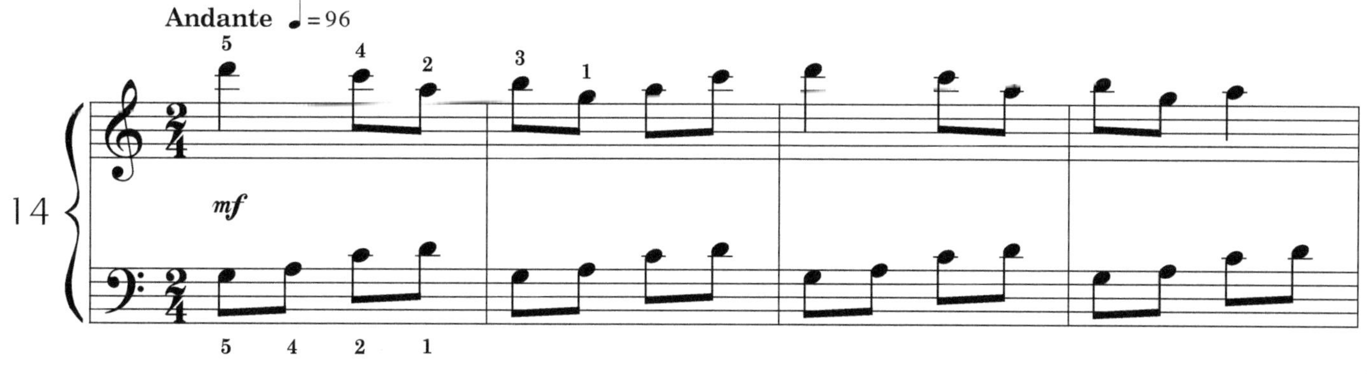

Andante ♩=96
mf

Andante ♩=96
mp
mf

Lentamente ♩. = 58 (♪ = 174)

16

Allegro ♩ + ♩. = 56 (♪ = 280)

17

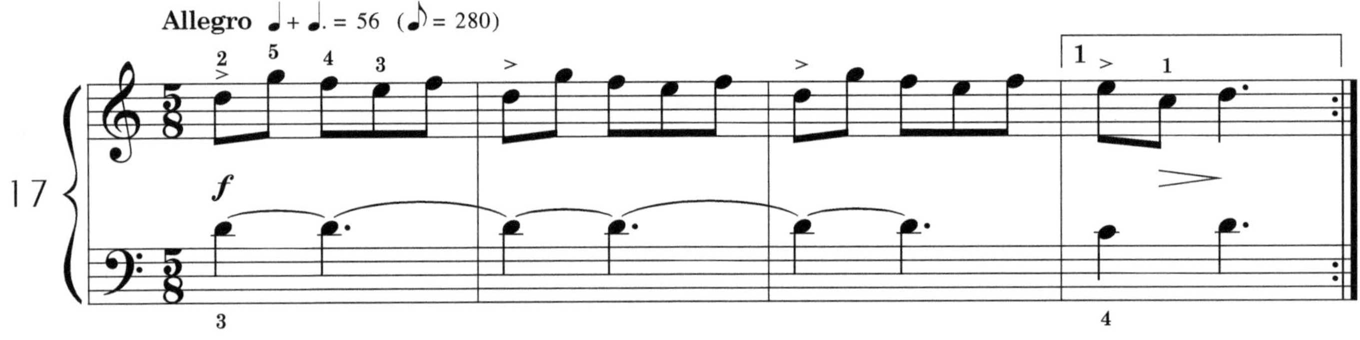

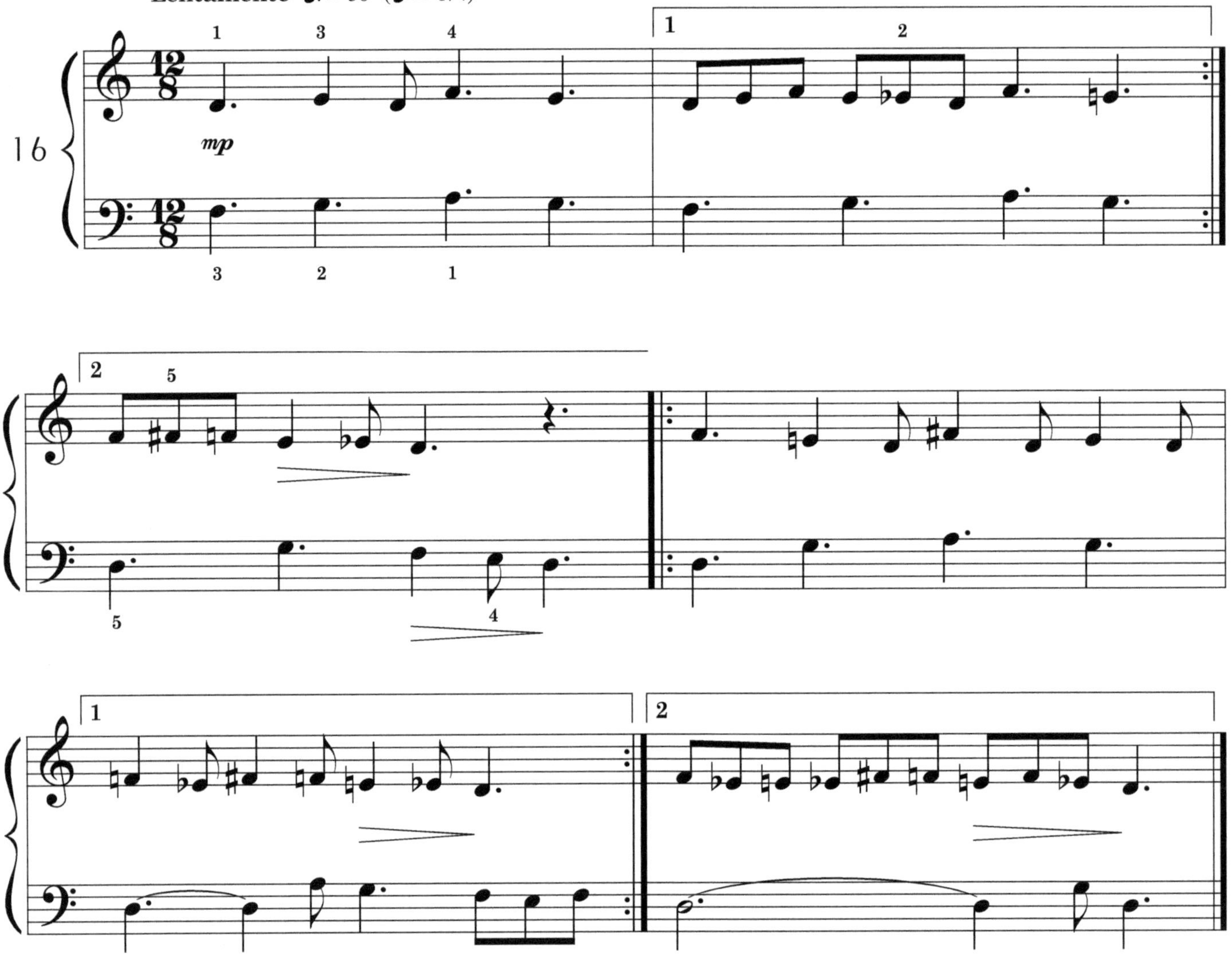

2
mf

f

Allegro
Fine
18
mp
f
D.C. al Fine

GA 22040

© 2017 - GA music

Allegretto
mf
21

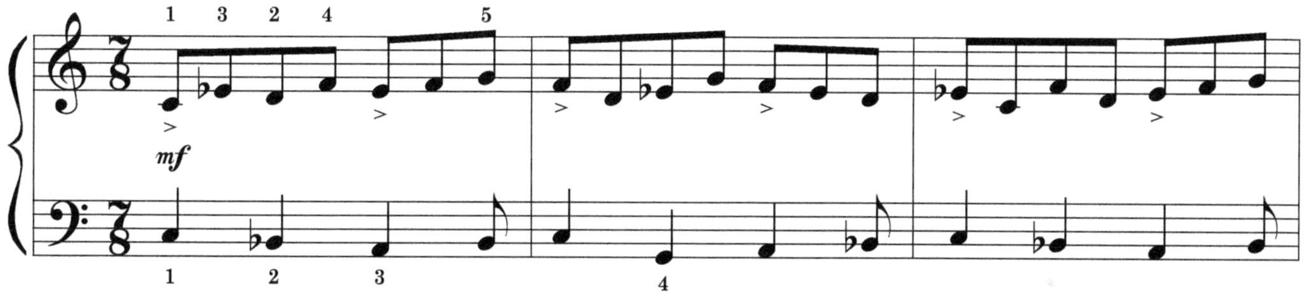

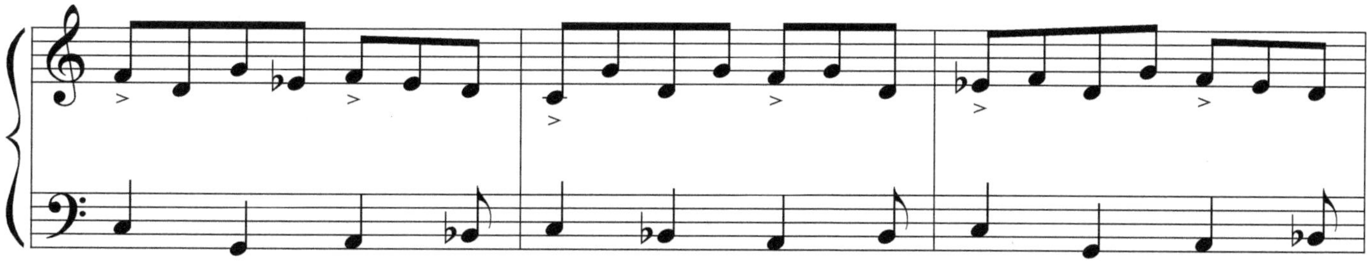

22
Andante ♩ = 100
f
5 2 4 3 1
1 4 5 2 3

p
f

23
Andante ♪ = 80
pp
5 1
mp
5 4 3 1 2 4
mf f p pp

GA 22040

Allegretto
24
25
Lentamente
mf
f
p
mf

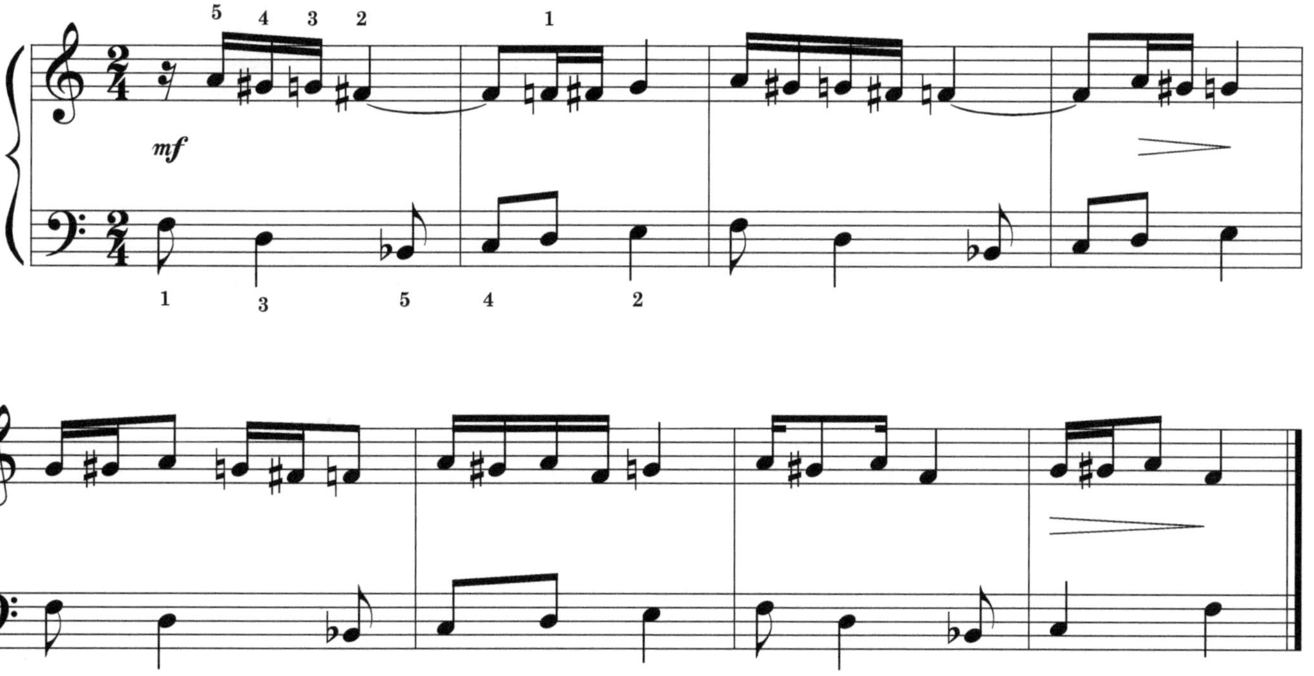

GA 22040

GA 22040
© 2017 - GA music

Lento ♩ = 58
32
mf
Calmo ♩. = 46 (♪ = 138)
33
mp

GA 22040
© 2017 - GA music

Calmo ♩. = 56 (♪ = 168)
mp
36
Presto ♩ = 192
mf
37
f

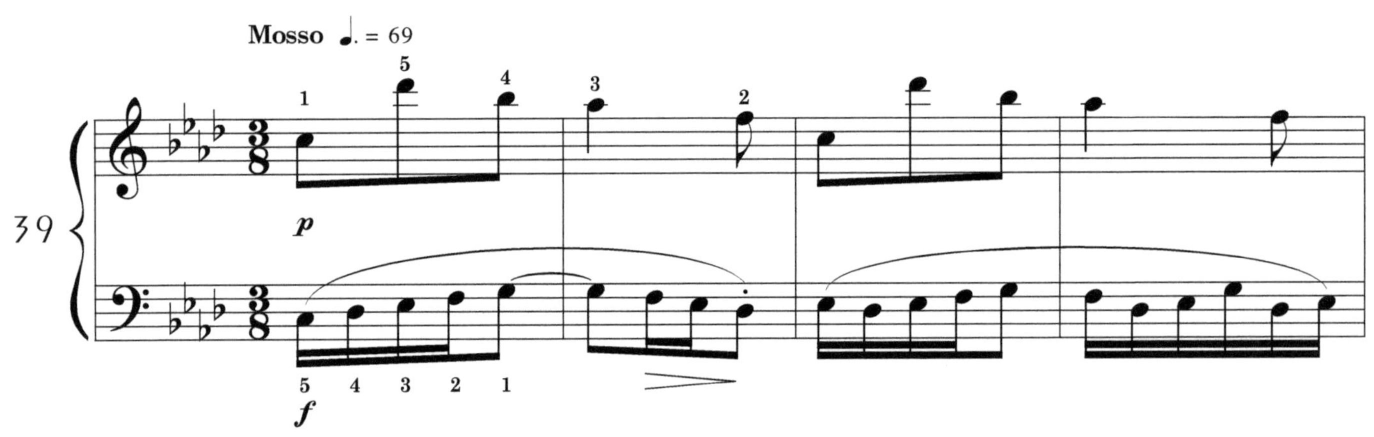

GA 22040

Allegro ♩ + ♩. = 38 (♪ = 266)
7/8
mf
1   2   3   4   5
3   5   2   4
40

f
1

ff

rit.
pp

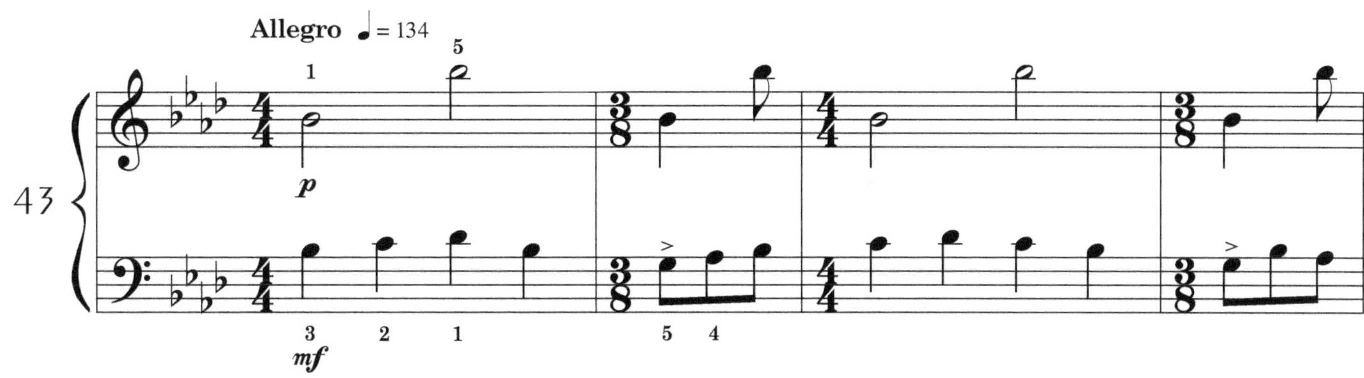

Allegro ♩ = 134
43
p
mf

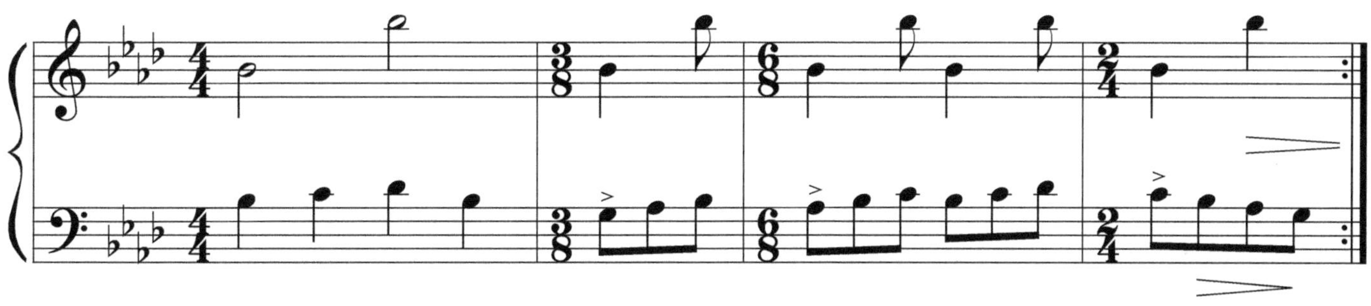

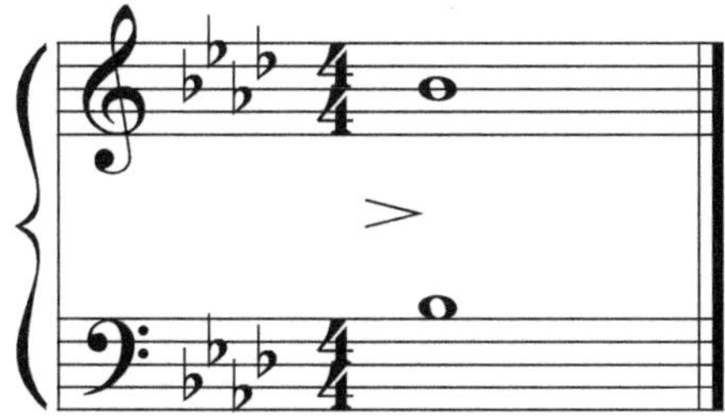

GA 22040

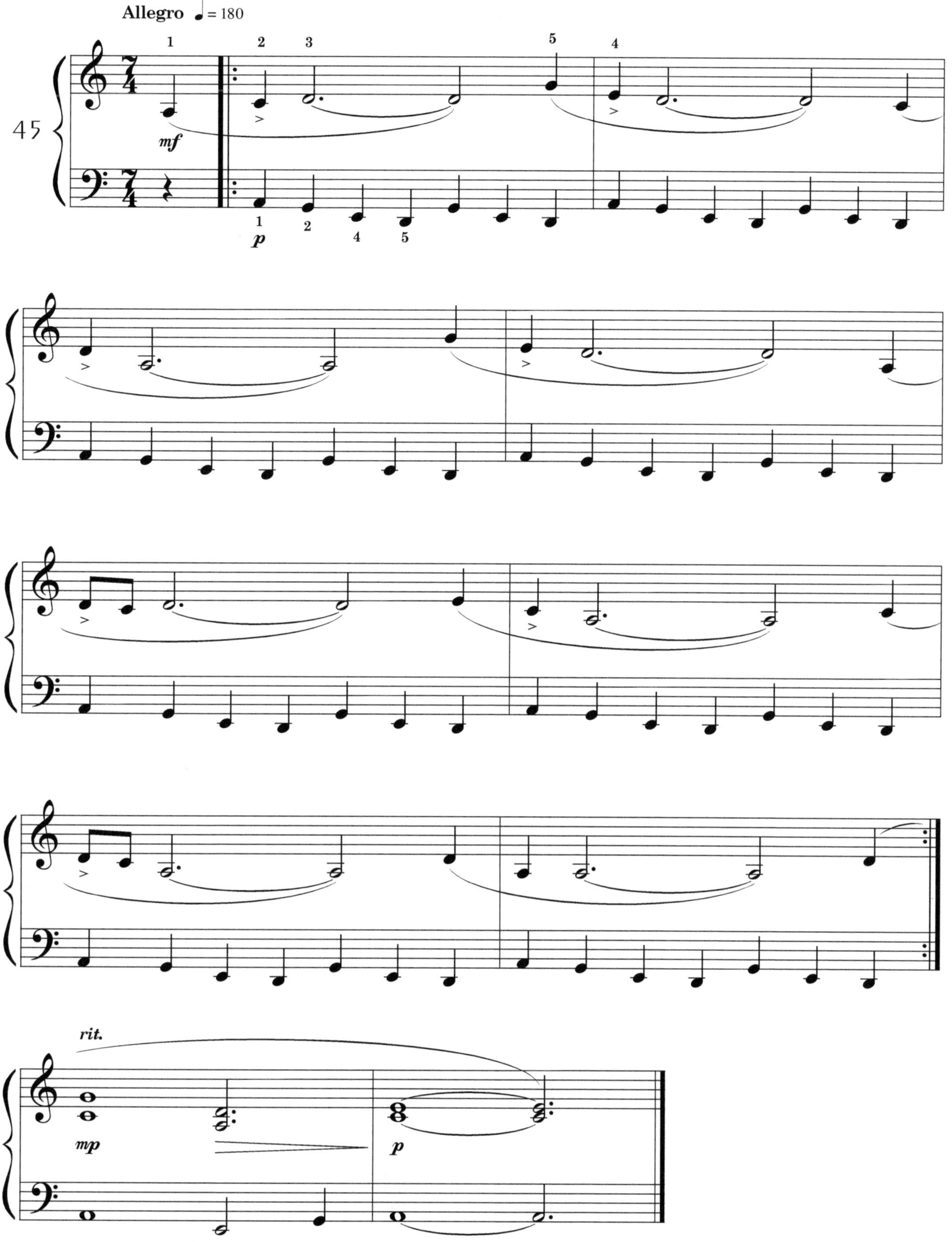
Allegro ♩ = 180
45
mf
p
rit.
mp
p

GA 22040

Lentamente ♪ = 106
47
pp
mp
1
5
1
2 3 4
5
rit.
ppp

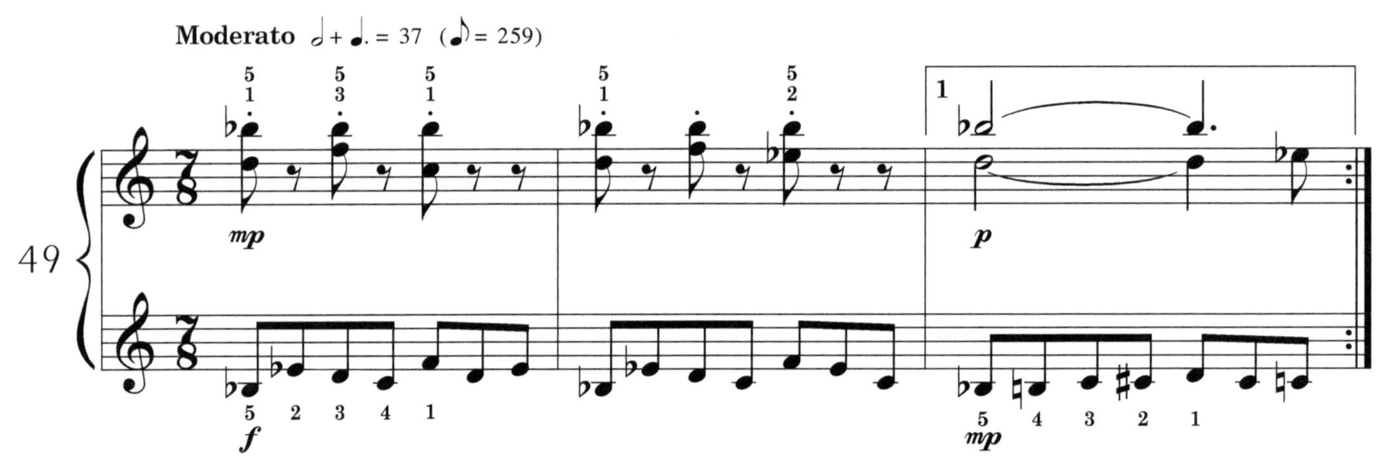

GA 22040

GA 22040

Allegro Moderato ♩ = 120
52
p
mf
rit.

Adagio
53
mp
p
GA 22040

Mosso ♩ = 160
54
f

GA 22040

www.ingramcontent.com/pod-product-compliance
Lightning Source LLC
LaVergne TN
LVHW071610180726
843512LV00003B/607